CARNIVAL

Joan Colby

FUTURECYCLE PRESS
www.futurecycle.org

Library of Congress Control Number: 2016948081

Copyright © 2016 Joan Colby
All Rights Reserved

Published by FutureCycle Press
Lexington, Kentucky, USA

ISBN 978-1-938853-91-3

*To my consummate editor
and dear friend, Diane Kistner*

Contents

CARNIVAL

SIDESHOWS

THE TRAVELING CIRCUS

CARNIVAL

Cotton Candy

A sugared web, too sweet.
Cloying words to seduce
With duplicity. Aftertaste
Stains the tongue the way a lie
Lingers to confuse.
Artificially pink as the flamingoes
On suburban lawns or the feet
Of mourning doves, their winsome offers,
Who, who is yearning? Pink as innerness,
As what opens
To sense, to love. A stick to lick at.
You have to want it
Because it's carnival—
An annual celebration
Of bad taste. The roof of the mouth
Sticky with clouds
As if angels wept.
And sated, you still can't finish
Those final glassy threads.
Too much, never enough.

Tilt-A-Whirl

To be queasy is how some people
Think of love. Vertigo of desire where
Being swung out of the ordinary
Dictates of balance is enough
To make you think the extraordinary
Will last beyond the mad impulse.
Infatuation, that's the dizzy specter
They said beware of. How what can't last
Can make you stumble as you exit
With the world still out of kilter,
Still spinning in its violent colors,
And look, look, how they line up
Holding their tickets, wanting
The experience of whirling until
The gorge rises in the throat.

Merry Go Round

The best horse is decorated with gold leaf
And rises up and down, not stationary
Like the ones for the littlest kids.
You race to get that one,
On the outside so everyone can see
How elegantly you ride,
Smiling, your tanned legs firm,
Your parents watching. The music
Of the calliope goes around
Repeatedly as the ride begins and ends.
It's the introduction to revolution,
How it proceeds, circular as eternity,
Or the image a child draws
Of the sun, its rays extruding
To applause.

Goldfish

What you wanted was to win
One of those glittery fish
In the little pond beneath the
Tent-flaps. Toss the ring
And, if you're lucky, a goldfish
Will be scooped into a plastic bag
Half-filled with water that you'll haul
All day, keeping up with the other kids,
Until your parents say it's time
And drive home. You're half-asleep.
The fish's gills still moving in and out.
Your mom buys some fish flakes at the grocery,
Which you bestow with generosity
For the week the goldfish lives.

Shooting Gallery

It's your dad who'll raise the rifle
To his shoulder in order to prove
His manhood to his daughters.
The rows of teddy bears and pandas
You have to have. He's a dead-eye shot,
He tells you. Scored high in the Marines
But not a sniper. He'll bust those bottles,
Wait and see. It might take all the cash
In his pockets, but he's never leaving
Without putting a big pink bear
In your arms. It's a lesson in perseverance
And love. Still, you have to think
What if he never does it. That could happen
And you know how he would sulk,
His underlip jutting as he drives home,
Not speaking to you, swearing at a
Car that cuts him off.

Monster Slide

What you do is climb
What seems a thousand steps
To the hyperbole of the slide
That rears over the whole shebang
Like a dinosaur.
A sort of towel is provided
To enhance your downward glide.
Hump after hump, gaining momentum,
You learn how angels fall
Into perdition when they challenge
The word made flesh. It's all
Over before you know it.

Face Painting

Stylized flowers or cartoon icons
Advertise readiness. The way
Indians applied war paint
To seal intention. The carny woman
Who adorns you is covered
With vines and roses.
An octopus winds up her left arm.
A bracelet of thorns on one wrist.
What might be a poem descends
Into the crack between her breasts.
For real? Asks a child, touching.
She smiles. *Wouldn't you like to?*

Daddy

Big burly guy like him, how can his kid
Be scared to ride the pony
Or the little airplanes cruising only feet
Above the ground. Crying *I don't want to*
When he offers to go with him
On the Tilt-A-Whirl. Not even the
Carousel. *See there. Babies go on it.*
The kid wails. He yanks him along.
You won't be getting a frozen custard.
The kid sobs. *I wanna go home.*
He shakes his head, despondent.
What's he done to get a son
Who quakes at everything. Who can't even
Understand what's fun.

Ferris Wheel

That boy, the one who invited risk,
Was the one who loosened the bar
As you stalled on the top, the one who started
Rocking the delicate cage while you screamed
For mercy. The world far below
Dizzied with your terror
And excitement. Your hand gripped his knee,
Pleading *stop* as he grinned and rocked harder,
The way he'd intend later in the car.
So you were warned. When the wheel started
Its final revolutions, when at last you halted
And stepped off shakily, taking his hand,
You already knew what would happen.

Fun House

Darkness and skeletons that popped
Out of niches. Tilting stairs
Whacked your balance. Mirrors
Fattened you like children in the forest
Or stretched you on the racks of distortion.
The boys could grope you
In the blindfolded tunnels,
You could pretend nothing went on.
Everyone laughed or screamed.
You slid down inclines,
Came face to face with coffins,
And ghosts waved spiderwebs
Over your arms. When you emerged
You weren't changed, just disheveled,
Denying propriety. The Mardi-Gras instant
Where everything is permitted.

Roustabout

Sweaty, swarthy in undershirt
And ripped jeans, needing a shave.
Shifty, still something sexy
In those bronzed muscles, that lean
Torso, grin that promised what you'd
Never imagined until now. *Hey, Red,*
He says, helping you into the seat
Of the wheel that will heft you skyward.
He leans too close fastening the bar
Over your bare thighs. The wheel lifts slowly.
All the people below shrink into
Another dimension. You are sixteen
And ready for this. Or maybe not.

Midway

Pockets jingling as they swagger
Between the rows of booths where hawkers
Challenge them to try their luck.
These boys need to impress the girls,
Oohing and aahing over tokens,
A necklace or something soft
And cuddly. A throwing arm
Or shooter's eye is what's needed.
And even though they know it's rigged,
They've got to try.
Ante up. Lose all you've got.
There'll be no cotton candy or root beer floats,
No ferris wheel hugging, nothing sweet
And sticky to remember. A guy with sideburns
Says, *Hey fella. That little girl wants to see*
Your pitch.

Feasts

Elephant ears, deep-fried, festooned with sugar,
A protected species of carnival,
Hot grease tanking the humid air
So breath seizes the way poison gas
Drenched the trenches. Still the mouth
Waters for succulence. Crisp and oil-
Laden as a pipeline to heart attack.
Ice cream floats like a bloated body
In the dark acid of root beer. It's good
To quench the thirst. Good as lemonade
Piss-sweet-sour in a paper cup. Ribs blacken
On vast grills manned
By sweating guys armed with prongs.
Hot dogs in poppy seed buns lavished
With mustard yellow as Vincent's sunflowers,
Cyanide piccalilli, shattered onions
Dripping in a cardboard coffin.
Explosions of cotton candy, pink
As ersatz flamingoes. Deep-fried
Snickers and cookie dough.
Chocolate-shelled bananas.
Everything sweet and greasy.
Flimsy napkins that can't cleanse
Your hands or mouth of wanting.

Dunking Tank

It used to be some black guy
Coerced with a few bucks who'd agree
To be the target on the seat
Over the tank. That's no longer
Considered cool. So it's the school
Principal who says every ball thrown
To drench him will raise the dough
For the new gym. The students line up
To send him floundering in his
Wool suit, again and again. How we love
To admonish authority. *See,*
You're no better than us or anybody.

Corn Boil

Homer Leinweber's steam engine
Fires the boiler. Hundreds of ears
Plumping sugared kernels
Of sweet corn. Slathered with
Butter and salt, you know this is the
Corn belt. Bellies boiling over
Belts, these men who know
What's good. *Line up. Bite in.*
He crumbles a fist of soil,
Wipes it on his tee shirt, says
See this black dirt. Best in the world
Here in the heartland.
High fructose corn syrup,
Rich enough to make your blood boil.

Shell Game

The pea
Hides beneath one of the shells.
You deliberate:
Left. Middle. Right.
Sinister. Conformity. Purification.
The choice should be simple
And never is. Trust gut or luck,
The inevitable odds
You can't decipher
While the pitchman chants.
Doomed like the unbaptized to a limbo
Of indecision, you hover like a hummingbird
While a crowd gathers
To egg you on. Ah, what is worse
Than a lousy guesser.
You hesitate, your fingers twitching
Like a dowser's forked branch. The pea
Hides beneath one of the shells
Or does it.

Bumper Cars

Everything you were taught to avoid:
Crashing, blocking, spinning out,
Deliberately jolting your best friends,
Laughing at their misfortune—
It's all permitted. You can drive
The red car of revenge,
Sideswipe the lover who cheated
And thought you'd never find out.
See his surprise as you aim once again
And stomp the pedal to the floor.

Daytime-Nighttime

Daytime, it's mom and dad and kids.
Sticky-faced toddlers, babies in strollers.
The carousel, the little cars,
Ponies tethered to a treadmill.
The sun blasts them; a little girl weeps
Over a fallen frozen custard. Her mother says
Shut that up or else we're leaving.
A grinning boy rides his dad's strong shoulders.

Nighttime's for teens. Tattooed and strutting
With belly rings and low-rise jeans.
Girls in wolf packs, eyeing possibilities.
Boys lounging with cigarettes
And weed for later. They cruise.
Promenading.
They text each other,
Take selfies.
The spirit of carnival says
Whatever.

Palm Reader

Two women with toddlers enter the tent.
The first is eager; the second hangs back.
Come on, says the first. *Aren't you curious?*
She thinks the future
Is in her hand. Extends it to the gypsy
Who offers the canned
Interpretations: lifeline, fateline, loveline.
Talent. Health. A man
Who might be faithful. A long journey.
Now, it's her turn, the dubious one.
She was a child when her mother died
Of cancer. That dark blemish that she
Fears. Asks the question. The gypsy pauses,
Holding her hand as if to comfort.
Prevaricates. *No one can say.*
But they can see the lifeline.
How it breaks off
Mid-palm. What does that mean?
The gypsy mutters. *It might not matter.*
The women turn to each other. To the
Children who cling to their skirts.

Senior Day

Half price. They arrive
Early. Skip the Midway for the
Flea Market. He paws tools like those
He has. She spies a china pattern
Just like Ma's. They linger over
Racks of paperbacks. Doilies someone's
Great-aunt crocheted. License plates from
Fifty states. An old guy who once rode
A Harley rolls on a Rascal or trudges
In a walker's cage. A frail woman hobbles on a cane
Or is wheeled like an infant
By a surly daughter-in-law. They attain
The tent where wares are hawked:
The magic brooms, the herbal weight-loss pills,
Elixirs to clean everything the way sin
Is scrubbed in confession, refrigerator magnets
Of the Lord's Prayer. A booth where a local
Politician hands out pamphlets praising his
Opinions. At noon they gather
In the tent for the pork chop dinner
And bingo. He visits the old tractors.
She buys salt and pepper shakers—two cunning piglets
For her collection.

Sideshow

It's better than being hid
In an attic, says the lizard woman.
Those genetics: midget, Siamese twins,
Pinheads, bearded woman, armless girl with
Educated toes, lobster boy, living skeleton,
Fat lady. Then those of deliberation:
Sword swallower, fire eater, snake charmer,
Tattooed man. It's a living.
Let the rubes pay to gape
At the extraordinary. The lizard woman says,
Being exceptional is easy money.
The cooch dancers grin.

Cooch Dancer

These old farmers.
The mystery of a woman's pussy.
Wives in flannel gowns
Insist on darkness.
Bachelors in filthy long johns
Crowd in closer. Grizzled,
Bearded, or scraped
Jaws. One man brought his son.
Sixteen is old enough. They can
Inseminate a cow. Pull a calf
With chains. It's not the same.
They've paid the extra dollar
For the Indian. The barker talks her up.
She teases, tossing garments,
Then struts to the edge of the stage,
Hands spreading her thighs. They lean in,
Lean in, shouting *Show me!*

Fire Eater

Lift the tong.
Now let your eyes glide up
In a saint's ecstasy.
Kiss it into flame
And tell those watchers how dangerous

This is, how long it took you
To learn the art of perfect
Breath control, how one slip

Instead of exhaling, breathing in
Means death in seconds. The lungs
A golden window with a child
Singing lullabies of the holocaust.

They lean in
To your spiel; you've got them.
Tilt your head back, the thrust

Extinguishing fire, then spit
The torch ablaze again. Hear them applaud?

You lick your lips.

The taste of burning
Haunts you. The children's eyes
Igniting like sticks.

Sword Swallower

Tell them the blades are dull.
Your candor leaves its mark.
Now they'll believe anything.
They'll believe no matter what you stick
Down that throat of yours won't hurt.

Don't tell them how long it took
To learn how not to choke.
The gag reflex, a kind of physical conscience,
Gone at last. No steel can
Make you flinch, even the serrated sword
That helps the crowd blanch.

You kneel as if to receive
A sacrament and let the blade
Coast through your gullet,
Easy does it. Like a ghost
You arise, the hilt of death
Jutting from your mouth.

Now slip it out slightly and smile.
They gasp as if you just drove
Devils out of hogs.
Three at once. You show
The knives. You take a bow
With blades still in place
Bending stiffly from the
Waist, it's all in knowing how.
The delicate angles.

The Storm

People throng the tents. Line up
For the Ferris Wheel, the Flying Swings,
The terrifying Parachute Drop.
Dark clouds spread wings
Across the western sky. Nobody stops
To look up until the sirens cry
Their raucous warning. *Come on,* says
One young dad, dragging his kids
Under canvas as the winds slam
Doors of rain. Hail big as eggs. They cower
Near tables set up for bingo.
The whole tent sails
Into darkness. He lies
Beneath a tent pole. The storm careens
Down the highway. Silence.
People pick through debris. A child
Pulls at her dad's limp hand.
Can we still go on the rides?

SIDESHOWS

Dorothy

They picked her out when the orphan train stopped.
She looked like a worker, a stocky girl,
Strong and solid. How wrong
They were. She went about singing,
Forgetting to feed the fowls
Or milk the cows. She burned
The bread and then the dreams
She persisted in telling. Silk hearts,
Cotton brains, wizards and such.
Lands sakes, he thought monkeys
Could fly. What's to be done
With such a girl? Then she ran off.
Just as well. It wasn't working
Out the way they'd thought.
But she came back to that wind-riven house,
That treeless prairie, the grey pair
With their puzzled, disapproving faces,
And she told them there are witches
And silver shoes and a man
Who'd turned to tin and a lion.
And then she sang and sang and sang
Until the whole sky
Darkened.

The Little Match Girl

All happy families alike just as
Lev declared. Gathered around the dinner table—
A crown roast, browned potatoes,
Eating, chatting, laughing—she
Watched them, a cold fire
In her heart, lonely, unfostered
In the dark of consequence. Flame
Anoints this absence, the two-story
Apartment seething gold at every window's
Mouth. The screaming of trapped
Children. She holds the can of
Gasoline, the box of matches—
How this scene warms her.
She awaits the sirens, the routine
Of ladders and hoses, smiles as though
Any of that could stop her.

Orphan Annie

Imagine Daddy Warbucks.
Only an orphan could be that lucky,
That vulnerable. The big stupid dog
Sandy could not guard her virtue
Or do anything but tag along
Scene to scene
As the balloons of her invocations
Sailed overhead. She got used to
Everything. Being kidnapped,
Held for ransom,
Listening to Daddy's wingnut philosophies,
His diatribes on the free market,
How little girls must be subservient.
Speechless Punjab was a relief.
Now she raises a fist. Her wild red hair,
Big round eyes empty as zeros.

Red Riding Hood

The age of innocence ends at seven.

First of all, the grandmother
With her ancient demands. The insistence
Of the aged to be honored. The woods
Were heavy with snow. All the trees
Bent over. If this was submission,
It was involuntary.

There must have been a mother who provided
What was to be offered. Who was torn
Between generations; their common enemy.
How she tried to appease them: the old woman
In her bed. The child ruddy with pleasure.

Everyone must have known what lurked
In the boundless places, sly and conniving.

Let us remember the child, too, was complicit.
Heedless, eager to go where she would not
Be commanded. Her red cloak in the forest.
Her basket of sweetness.

Rose Red to Snow White

A dark wind batters the door.
Our minds unchink as
The chimney roars and the eaves
Shriek in their rusty dreams.
Huddle by the fire, sister.
Something is snapping in the applewood,
And sparks ignite our nightgowns.
Let us save each other.
Let us marry these ashes.
Don't leave the comfort we've found
For that rap on the doorjamb.
God knows who'd be out
On such a night, in a blizzard
Like this one. Have no pity
On travelers far from town
In this fierce weather.
But you've unlatched us,
Let a whirlwind of white flakes
Confuse our destinies
And succored a brute of fur
Whose snout embeds
In your fabulous hair.
A thorn stabs
My red heart
As you lie down
With the great bear,
Bringing him to life
With your white body.
How can you be sure
He'll turn at last into something
Noble, that he won't always
Raid your breasts for honey
Or sleep grunting all winter?

Rapunzel

A golden fall, it grew and grew:
Admired, desired, then stalked
In the tower of jealousy.

You could have sheared it
But no one would have wanted you enough
To imprison. Did that sort of love transfix you,
Combing long strands
Over your hips?

When did the window of your room
Shrink so that the little light
That entered wasn't enough? You heard a voice
Calling, and you called back,
Deploying your sun-colored braid
Like a ladder that could free you
Or betray you.

Heidi

Artisanal anything, of course
She embraced that. Goat cheese,
Stone-milled breads. The hands-on
Curative diet. She never sleepwalks now
In the ebullient cities, exhaling the thinnest air.
When her party attacked Everest, she
Was the single oxygen-free survivor.
She is reminded
Of Grandfather, his rough hands,
The wisdom of his passion. Listen, orphans.
Know what it means to be chosen,
To pluck the edelweiss in the
Highest pastures above the timberline
Where everything precious can be touched.

Goldilocks

Good looking, smart, well-spoken. You'd think
She'd choose. But always
She discovered the flaw.
On Match.com, any man
Viewing her profile would think *This woman*
Could be the one. She needled out the wrong
Phrase or how he dressed
Inappropriately. His receding
Hairline, incipient beer belly, how his buttocks
Sagged like beagles' ears, his teeth
Yellow as old maps. He could be a
Womanizer prowling the World Wide Web
With a fictitious bio and sweet talk.
She could never trust.
It went way back, but *You*
Don't need to know that story
Is what she told him with a grimace
Over coffee. She hardly ever got
To the point of dinner and he, of course, expected—
As all of them did—sex.
What she was after wasn't that.
Not love, not companionship,
Not the commercial where they giggle
And touch each other and hold hands,
Two happy Christians who'd learned how to pick.

Raggedy Ann and Andy

She has a pinafore and red yarn hair.
He wears blue overalls and a snug cap.
They both have button eyes
And sewn-on smiles.

They could be fraternal twins
Or a married couple. See how they recline
With long-practiced ease
On the patchwork quilt.

Well-traveled with a camel, faded white
In Saharan suns, its knees collapsed beneath
Their well-stuffed torsos. The Raggedys
Hand in hand for adventure. Their never-changing

Expressions of approval no matter what
The yellow-haired fairy brandished
Or how surrounded
By pirates with hideous red

Sea-slug noses. The tired old horse
Could never carry them to safety.
They sit in bedside chairs
Where a weary child

Wishes their book shut,
Their floppy limbs deposited
Elsewhere.

Cinderella

There is no happily-ever-after.
That's what she learned. He tells her
What a prince he is and she
Believes it. He buys her four-hundred-dollar
Shoes and a mansion. But she has to account
For her whereabouts. He checks her phone
For texts, says it's because he loves her
Even though she was nothing
But a trashy slut whose stepmother
Beat her. She was lucky
He came along. *Think about that,*
He says. *Don't make me mad.*
I don't want to have to hurt you.

Sleeping Beauty

A spell procured
From old women for a price.
In his arms she is heavy,
Her loins gilt as constancy,
Breasts like sacks of money.

She sleeps in the tower
Of his desire. Until his final kiss
Like a wasp's sting shocks her
Upright, staring: Who is this man
Buckling his belt and grinning?

Mermaids

They dreamed of sirens whose haunting arias
Could whisk them willingly to oblivion,
Shipwrecked with lust. Who would resist the chance,
Roped to the mast like Odysseus, to risk
The heightened edge of consciousness—
Not quite blacked out but almost.
Any seal or manatee might be a mermaid
Willing to trade her tail for love
Or money like the whores in the gaudy ports.
Tales of women like flying fish
Skimming the waves to flop
Spread-eagled on deck. Longing
For beauty, they settled for buggery.
A notion of water sprites immured them
In the hammocks of tossed nights
When it seemed that land would never
Be sighted, that the maps promised dragons,
This voyage the last one.
Shanghaied, they sailed
The seven seas of imagination
Keelhauled with a ration of rum
And hardtack. The brutal lash,
The numb days of stagnation
When any story was better than none.

Wonder Woman

Laser-blue of her gaze
Confounds the evildoers.
Flying the invisible plane
Of her resolve, she lassos truth
From liars. The supermen of
Justice confirm her as secretary.
To serve coffee. To answer phones.
She kicks up her heels
In tight scarlet boots, leggy and determined
As the girl secretly reading
Forbidden comics in the basement
Of a city bungalow.

Years later, when that girl learns
She will lose a breast, she remembers
The Amazons sliced off
One pendulous tit to enable
The tendon of the bow to tighten.
That page where a woman grips with
Silver gauntlets and stands spread-legged.
The scar she'll bear as testament
To her singular wonder.

Mari Ruadh

She did not prick her finger
To fall asleep for a hundred years
Awaiting a kiss. She did not lose her slipper
To crouch humbly in the ashes
Awaiting rescue.

She was The Giant's daughter. She would choose
The man she wanted. Naturally, a prince.
As he quavered at the task
Her father set, she sang him to sleep,
Called the blackbirds
To thatch the barn.

He woke to climb a ladder
Of her fingers. She caressed him
Until her smallest digit rooted
In a tree. *This is how you'll know me,*
She said, holding up her ruined hand.

She stood with her sisters,
As if in a brothel, to be selected
And he chose her as she had directed.

They fled on a magic filly
With her father in pursuit.
Mari Ruadh plucked a twig
From the horse's ear and a forest grew.
She threw a pebble to build a mountain range,
A flask of water for a tsunami
That sucked The Giant far out to sea.
She laughed to see her father
Go down the final time.

The prince then forgot her, as men
Are wont to do. She conjured doves
Of gold and silver to peck his memory.

It was always her: maneuvering, insisting,
Saddling the horse. She'd never sit on a glass hill
Awaiting her fortune. She knew
What she wanted, and if she had to kill
The giant shadow of her sire, she would.

She would sacrifice her finger, sing
In the darkest wood, enchant the apples to lie,
The shoemaker to bless her, the well
To hold her reflection, the prince
To always love her
Or be sorry.

Brenda Starr

Stars glittered in the red chiffon
Of Brenda's hair, in her emerald eyes.
A glamour girl, she stalked stories,
A mystery man with a continental patch.

He was always seeking
A black orchid in the heart of Brazil
That would keep him from losing
His mind. Brenda would begin
To forget him, riding in the white convertible
Of a boyish entrepreneur when the invidious
Odor of black orchids would overtake her.

Thus it was she pursued a career,
Never growing older, never learning
Nothing would change. She befriended
The fat and the homely, typical foils
For beauty. Each had a quirk. Brenda
Went after the story. She went
To the ends of the earth,
Red-haired as a witch,
Her stockings unrun in the Andes,
Her spike heels unscuffed in Afghanistan.

She interviewed the Sphinx as to the locale
Of orchids, the black ones that calm madness,
Make love a possibility. She mounted a camel
Wearing a tailored safari-outfit,
Her hair caught in a snood.

Meanwhile the mystery man was steaming
Down the Nile on his endless mission.
He was destined to run into Brenda
Whose surprise was to be expected
As she could never see past the panel
That held her adventures.

A balloon rose over her head
Containing the things that she said
Or, lacking a hook, what she thought.
She yearned for the mystery man,
A suit by Chanel, a scoop.

Mary Mallon

All I know is cooking.
It is not my fault. The germs they say I harbor
In my gallbladder of all places.
I won't succumb to the knife.
I find another place where they
Appreciate my skill: the stews,
The soups, the Sunday roasts,
My excellent apple pies. Be damned
To them, the rogues who would
Govern my life, the constables
Who insist I wash my hands. I'm a clean
Woman, big and strong. Healthy as a horse.
They made me scrub in a hospital laundry,
A woman whose devil food cake
Could water your mouth with desire.
How could I, never sick a day,
Sicken others. That quack Soper
Wanted to look at my shit. I shook
The cleaver in his face until they
Seized me, but I ran
Like a red heifer from the slaughterman,
Ran for five years. They claim people died.
People I fed. Who ate my cooking with relish.

Belle Gunness

She threw her false teeth into the flames
And vanished.

Later her lover, Lamphere, told his cellmate
That it wasn't Belle's corpse the police found
But that of a vagrant woman lured to the farm.

Triflers need not apply. Belle's ads ran
In the Chicago papers. She yearned for a sincere man,
The one all the widows pine for.
Fourteen of them responded and disappeared.
Belle butchered them like hogs,
Skinned off their greenbacks.

In April 1908 the farm burned.
Dismembered bodies in the pigpen.
It is said she drugged them first.
The last thing they dreamed of was her embrace.
Was she beautiful? The body in the ashes headless,
Said not to be hers at all. She vanished

With a stuffed wallet
Or else she died there screaming black-faced
With her children.

Lamphere always said
It wasn't Belle. He died in the Indiana pen
Still professing
She threw her false
Teeth into the flames and vanished.

Pandora

The child can't resist finding out
What the wrapped box in the
Closet holds. A spoiled Christmas
Of faked surprise—not even
What she really wanted.
Ten years married—the ritualistic
Sexual act just as he likes it. Her mind roves
Ghostly on a distant planet.
The affair begins like that,
Her heart opening like a treasure chest
Filled with butterflies. This lasts
A little while. The rendezvous
In seedy motels, surreptitious dinners,
The dirty weekend camouflaged
As a business trip. It all becomes
Routine. The he-says, she-says.
Infection feasts upon her boredom.
She jiggles the lid
Chancing discovery.

Medea

The children drowned
In the bathtub. She lay
On the bed with the capsules.
Unable to complete the circle.

Or the car shoved
Into the lake, the hands of the
Small boys waving
From the rear window. Now she
Was free.

After she served the meal
And he had eaten
And she described the recipe—
So went the story, though
Euripides says she simply
Slaughtered them so he could see
The blood oozing beneath the doorsill—

She wrote his name
In their blood.
The man whose disdain
Or abandonment was the fault
In the earth beneath the red
Clay of her fury.

Three Brothers

The story begins.
There are three wishes.
Three princes.

The eldest must perform an impossible task.
To set an example,
He perishes.

The middle one
Shuts his book of platitudes
And rides into the legends
Of fire breathers and snake-coifed women
Who turn their lovers to stone.

The youngest,
Simple-minded and covered with ashes,
Gawks from his cross-legged
Pose by the fire
And stalks into a roundelay with chance.

His great fortune
Is trusting the most
Connived-at circumstance.
Guileless, he takes
Life at face value.

When he meets the dragon,
He is armed with the dusty charms
Of the hag in the cave of the winds:
The golden feather, the bone, the jeweled pin
From the hair of the real princess.

Chosen one, God's fool.
Towers crumble under the stride
Of his seven-league boots

As he blindly staggers
Into each parable whirling the sword
Of belief in his own star.

The epilogue of happily-ever-after?
There is no moral to this tale.
Even now, some brute
Is rising from his pallet.

Huck Finn

Settled in a sod house in Kansas,
Plowing the tough soil with a
Mule named Jim. Or celestially wed
To three Mormon women,
A passel of tow-headed children
Calling him Father. Or did he get as far
As San Francisco, sharp at cards
Or tinkling the piano keys in a bordello.
Was he one of the Buffalo hunters
Blackening the plains with hides,
Did a Sioux woman bed him,
Did he break mustangs for the cavalry
Or ride shotgun on the stage to Cheyenne.
Did he ever reminisce about the widow
Or Tom, intruder of a final chapter,
The Shepherdson's inexorable feuds,
The Dauphin and the Duke. Did he peddle
Patent medicines from a wagon bed.
Is there a stone on the high prairie
With his name and date. Did he end up
Like Pap, drunk on a riverbank,
With his son cursing a memory
Of beatings and deception.

Tom Sawyer

A judge now, having read
Law, married Becky, settled in a fine house
Overlooking the Mississippi. Gruff
In a three-piece worsted, a Derby
And a gold watch, fob and chain.
Harrumphs at those gaudy rumors
Of airships and African adventures.
Frowns at rude schoolboys. He knows
Their game. The practiced trickery
Of smart alecs, their whitewashed
Duplicities. Authorizes the padlocks
For that terrifying cave where once he
And Becky wandered with their candles
Guttering as love does over the years.
He never speaks of the bloody fingerprints
Where the Indian scrabbled for light.
Carves his Sunday roast
And presides.

Woodman

Bearded visage, axe, he comes to the rescue
Of the children fleeing the candy house,
The cloying call,
The ovens.

He tramps the dark forest where they
Scattered bread crumbs that ravens devoured,
Where their footsteps led further and further
Into the mystery of loss. How they were invited
By evil, saved by imitation.

Alone, the tree trunks closing in as if the world had
Shrunk into the scope of two hands.
Always the woodman.
Once he killed a deer to take its heart
As proof. Another child saved
For a prince's lust.

These too will be returned.
He gestures; they follow:
Brother, sister, trusting in a hut with a glad father.
How easily they forget the woman who said
Leave them. How, as they wandered,
Their cries were mistaken for
Owlets or nightjars.

When you lose yourself, the woodman
Moves out of shadows
To escort you. *This way,*
He says.

Genie

Those three infernal wishes.

Giant with patience, he waits,
Turban nodding as this lucky one deliberates.
Wealth, health, or love.
He foresees the mistake.
How the wish should be:
More wishes. He'd supply
An infinity of wants.

Yet he is again
Disappointed. In a plume of blue smoke
Retreats into the vessel
Of burning oil. The power of giving
Is always resented. The wrong choices
That keep him imprisoned
In the shining jar.

Mowgli

A small man in suit and tie,
His voice pitched soft so the
Audience leans forward, intent.
He advises attention
To nuance, to body language:
What is unsaid is the most important.
Think of a bear. Wise and kindly.
Don't be fooled by monkey-
Shines. As for snakes, they can't be
Trusted. All that hissing. All that poison.
Cleanse your life of this. Understand
You'll only value what you pay for.
Beware of those who never were fed
By wolves, who never felt the incisors
On their necks sinking in with love.
It's that language you must learn.
When the tiger approaches the village,
It's you he's singled out. I give you now
A word to hum
Over and over with conviction.

Count Dracula

Hair oil, a center part, zinc oxide
To whiten the complexion. Lips
Carmine, evening wear, bow tie
(Omit the silver cufflinks),
Bat-collared cloak to spread aloft
When landing on the balcony
Where a pale blonde in a negligee trance
Awaits the fanged kiss.

A full moon grazes on a field
Of black moire. Arrogance is also
Required and composure
As the windows of the innocent
Swing open. And dancing pumps,
A riveting stare across that
Cliché of crowded rooms. Daylight
Is to be avoided, and forget confessions
Of the coffin, the chambered cellar
Or the curse of the undying. You know
The ending: a good man
With a cross and a pistol with one
Dazzling bullet and his companion,
The old and kindly doctor
Who wields the stake.

Was it worth the disguises, you may ask,
The bone-rattling coach ride through
The mountains of Transylvania, the peasants
And their platitudinous torches? A little blood,
A little fame, the late show
Where you styled upon the staircase
Haughtily, awaiting an introduction.

Wallenda

The windy city in blustery November
Is what he's chosen, desiring like Houdini
The drama of the unattainable.

Cables strung between Marina Towers,
Two wedding cakes of glass and steel,
A difficult placement for right-angled

Dwellers, but he's struck with the motif:
Midwestern schmaltz inviting round beds
Reminiscent of the center ring

Where his forefathers erected human pyramids
In vaulted air and learned the sentence
Of failure could be irrevocable.

A triple feat is what he's devised:
Another wire stretched across the river
To a skyscraper square as the equation

He plans to solve. Famous as a wind tunnel,
This route will test the nerve
Of trembling watchers

Whose challenge,
Like his, is what
In the world they long for.

Floyd Collins

Wedged like that. In a crevice underground.
Hands trapped at his sides.
He shaped himself wormlike to wiggle
Through the corkscrews that worked until
A pitbull rock dislodged to seize and hold his ankle.

He'd spent a lifetime in these caves. It wasn't as if
He didn't know his trade. The thrill of discovery,
A hall of glittering stalactites and gypsum flowers.
This time had been a disappointment. A dark
Smoked cavern with no enhancements. He was
On the way out when it happened.

Three days waiting. Then the relief of voices.
They'd dig away the gravel that
Kept sifting, somehow slide his body from
This coffin. The story is famous. Thousands gathered
Around bonfires, eating and drinking. The newsmen
Had a heyday. All the while he suffered
And hoped, which was the worst.

Maybe he gave up when another cave-in
Blocked access and he could no longer see
Anything. How he must have felt
In that underworld. You know how
This ends. They sank a shaft too late,
And even then they couldn't retrieve him.

Imagine being wedged, rocks gripping you so tight
You can hardly breathe, much less move
A finger or turn your head. Trapped
Like a sausage in a petrified bun,
A knife in a rusted sheath,
A key in a frozen lock. The limestone
Fit his body like a suit of underwear,
As if all these years this spot had carved itself
To await his coming.

Poirot and Marple

They never met.
She: a chatty old lady, rather kindly,
Beloved by all but the wicked.
Those analogies to village events:
How someone's maid served the tea
Corresponding with how the murderer was obsequious.

He revered the little grey cells
That, like factory workers, concocted
A resolution that he'd elaborate
At last in the drawing room
With everyone assembled.

Her victims succumbed on trolleys,
In libraries or the vicarage.
His elected a manor,
A seaside house party
Or a dig in Assyria.

He traveled: the Orient Express,
A cruise down the Nile.
She rarely journeyed farther
Than Bertram's Hotel, preferring
To stay home in St. Mary's Mead.

Neither could solve the mystery
Of Agatha's disappearance:
*Amnesia. The signature in the name
Of her husband's mistress.*

Imagine the interview:
Agatha says she can't remember.

Madame! He chortles, fixing
The monocle in his eye. She whispers
My dear! and pats Agatha's hand.

Click of knitting needles.
Twirl of the moustache.

Enchantments

Changing into stone is never swift
But operates according to the slow
Law of petrification.
The process of replacing sentience
With calcification is happening all the while
Beneath your notice.

Changing into the beast
Is terrible. Suddenly speech is absent,
The way of looking lowered,
Until hunger and lust assume dimensions
More intense but less interesting. The pupils
Of your eyes are oblongs or slits. The hair on your neck rises.
Your pelt fits
Loosely over the musculature and the long
Preambles of love are meaningless.

Celtic Demons

The Dullahan

The black horse snorts,
Eyes burning coals,
Hoofs striking sparks from
The tarred roads. It's moonlight,
Of course, when he rides, severed head
Tucked under the arm of his
Greatcoat. The swags of blood he
Throws from his iron bucket will
Condemn you. Look aside,
Sojourner. Hold up your cross of gold.

Balor

A single eye
To concentrate his purpose.
Wide, lidless, the pupil
Like a bullet slays by staring.
One giant leg like Long John Silver's
To leap the hedges where the living
Hide. Staring and stomping
Through the nightmares of children
Until they fall into the deeps
Of dreams where his water demons ride.

Kelpie

Ghost horse, its seaweed mane dripping
With saltwater, with the tears
Of the unbaptized. Beware
Of a steed captured so easily,
How it bends its head into the bridle,
How it canters metrically
To rock you into the sleep
Of the seas you enter, the dark
Waters you will breathe.

Leanan Sidhe

Muse of poets and singers,
Harpists and rhymers,
Where does it come from,
The vision and the notion?
She smiles as you lift pen
Or bow, as the ink or the
Music unfolds its calligraphy.
How you wait for her shadow
To beautify your expectancy.
She paints her face with the blood
Of your efforts and strides the avenues
Seeking new talent.

Sluagh

Here come the dead sinners
In a murmuration of starlings,
Their wings darkening the western skies.
They nest in the hearts of those who remember,
In the guilt-house of the survivor.
Shut the windows where the dying lie
Reciting their final contritions.
Unabsolved, the sluagh open their beaks
To swallow the escaping spirits.

The Banshee

Hag in a fog-drenched robe
Or a beautiful redhead, her hood
Thrown back, her fire eyes blazing.
Keening a prophecy of the
Soon-to-be-dead. In the sod hut they stare
At each other, wondering.

Each Irish family owned one.
They crept on the coffin ships
Wrapped in shawls of woe.

The old tales slipped from the grandmothers' tongues
And were forgotten.

On winter nights, I hear that
Keening. There are strange tracks in the snow.
The hunger moon is overhead.
I thought it must be coyotes.
Even so.

The Alchemist

The shaft leads down
To the mother lode
In the mountains of the High Mojave.

Half a lifetime this prospector
Chiseled brute rock
Seeking traces
Of everything secret and precarious.

I must have walked over it
Hundreds of times. Then the vision
Drew me as water transfixes
A witch. My body has become
A dowsing stick. The soles
Of my feet burn with veins
Of gold and silver
Threading the earth's dark heart.

In a dirt-floored cabin,
He lives still
With a bible and a passel
Of cats. The desert wind
Wails day and night. The sun's doubloon
Shimmers. Sidewinders of dust waver
In the sacred ritual of noon.

He has charted this fault
With the conviction of a saint.
Geologists nod. Half silver, half gold,
The vein will yield a fortune.
The secular and industrious
Will root it out.
Amphisbaena, the fabulous beast,
Keeper of the great
Secret of commerce,
Will devour and spew each gain
From opposite mouths.

But all of this
Is immaterial to the prospector
Squatting in blazing light,
His body glinting,
Unkempt silvered hair.
How long he has been turning
Baseness into richness?

He says
This find will not change me.

Vampires

Examine history, how drinking the blood
Of an enemy or devouring his heart
Enriches your destiny. Kneeling at the altar,
You accept the flesh of Christ and swill
The wine of his veins. You have fasted
For this extraordinary transubstantiation
Just as Vlad the Impaler gloated
Over the stakes adorned with victims.
It's the idea of the undead, not the blood-lust
Or the coffin in the bowels of a ship
Or the fair-haired woman in a negligee
And an open window centered with the moon.
It's the power of night sojourners:
The owls' silent swoop, the bats' radar,
The wolf pack running in the snow
After a troika pulled by black horses.

Zombies

Drums tattoo the crossroads,
A cock's throat is slit,
A goat led forth where
Baron Samedi, in black top hat,
Shows his white visage in what might be
A smile or rictus. A woman dances stripped
As the denuded hills of Haiti.
Baron Samedi smokes a big cigar.

In Miami, a crazed man
Chews off the face of one too dazed
Or drunk to do more than scream.
He growls like a werewolf and is
Gunned down.

In New Orleans, another bites
A peach-sized chunk from
Someone's cheek. Subdued with
Wasp repellant, he draws a knife
That gleams like Baron Samedi's grin.

Intoxicated on Demon Passion Smoke
Or Voodoo Spice. Lungsful of Blue
Egyptian Water Lily, Indian Warrior,
Dwarf Skullcap.

The blue-eyed corpse arises
To march ashen-faced to the
Drumbeat of horror movies
As a child squeezes shut his eyes
And Baron Samedi laughs.

Superstitions

Napoleon exchanged his lucky scarab
For the hand of Marie Louise.
His star of destiny flared
Red as war to shatter
Like the crockery
Of Ulysses Grant's dream
Of prosperity. Dr. Johnson
Hopped pavement cracks, caressed lampposts.
A circle of amber
Fallen from paradise in the time of Mohammed
Rendered the Shah of Persia invisible
To conspirators against his throne.
Humbert the First had a bracelet
Set with three bezoar stones
That saved him from all
But the last assassin. Byron
Set sail on unlucky Friday
To die with his veins afire in Missolonghi.

Ghosts inhabit your dreams. They talk.
Their faces deny corruption.
A knife and fork
Cross on your plate. Salt
Spills. You walk
Under a ladder, smash mirrors
With a glance.

What do you need to live?
New moon over your right shoulder,
A pin, a four-leaf clover,
A horseshoe, knocking your luck
Into the wood's grain,
Sealing your wish
With the heart's scarlet wax,

Stealing a hairpin
From a red-headed woman,
Twining the stems of two sweetheart roses.

When a dog howls at your door,
You're done for. Bells toll
In your ears. The Archangel Michael
Opens his mouth of scissors.
Your eyes close
With money. Clocks stop.

Carnies

Found dead on the lawn of a rented house.
No I.D. The neighbors testify
Those carnies were living here last week.
Fights. Beer bottles in the yard.
They're long-gone now. The operator says
Guys sign on, we never know
Who's who. This one turns out
To be from Mississippi. Thirty-five years old,
String of minor infractions. There were three or four
Staying here. Rough types. It goes unsolved.
Nobody's pushing for justice—some outsider
Just as bad, no doubt, as whoever stabbed him.

Hamelin

Overrun with vermin,
The grain devoured.
Contaminated with black lozenges,
The rank piss of the invader.
They starved. *Who to*
Nourish—children or workingmen?
No need to feed the old. They shrink
Flesh to bone, cadavers of
Silence. The houses grew cold.
Cutting wood ate calories. They slept
In the hard beds of privation
Listening to the rustle of the rats
In the eaves. Small glittering eyes
Like penny nails. Voracious.
The angel arrived in the guise
Of a troubadour, pipes and mandolin
Slung over his shoulder. He
Made the deal that God allows:
This for that. They weighed the choices—
Kids or rats. What they saw were
Mouths. The interminable feeding.
After he'd led the rats off
In a long snake of furred tribulation,
They pondered. Go back on a vow?
Then what—damnation? It has always been
The old versus the young with their good
Molars, their appetite for more.
A parliament of judges deliberated
While the children rollicked. Heedless
And demanding. A story began: How a land
Of plenty existed, blessed with cherry blossoms,
Peavines and olives. The angel that drove them forth
Years and years ago has come back
With celestial music, a lyric of harmony.
The children listened spellbound
And began to pack for the diaspora.

THE TRAVELING CIRCUS

Circus Parade

Blasting frenzy, the calliope
Advances the Dionysian season.
Gold and scarlet wagons
Pulled by matched teams of Percherons.
Sequined ladies on white stallions
Or waving from the elephants' jeweled howdahs.
Bands of acrobats and trapeze artists,
Clowns and dancing dogs, barred cages
Of tigers and lions.
Shining instruments of the brass band.
The ringmaster's formal masquerade.
The streets of small towns
Lined with proper citizens
Prepared to pay
To be astonished.

The Greatest Show on Earth

In the devil's circus the clowns rule
With lipsticked grimaces and
Chalked demeanors, lure
Children to a three-ringed
Enchantment of how many can be crammed
Into the tiny vehicle of self-immolation.
Small dogs in tutus gambol
With the threat of whips secreted
Backstage, the box of treats
Offered as the popcorn vendors
Patrol the aisles of imagination.

Bad dreams convulse them in their beds,
Rendering yesterday's performance
In all its gilt and fakery: How the
Aerialist dangled by her knees
From the swinging bar of the trapeze,
Netless, nothing but a pair of powdered hands
Waiting for the catch and the release.

Ringmaster

Top hat and tails,
Polished boots. That's how
God would enter. Confident
In his power to whip
Ensembles into action.
His smile. His bow. His greeting.
He runs the show despite
The arrogance of the highflyers,
The rhinestone ladies on white horses,
The strutting clowns, the men in tights.
He's got pizazz. Announces
Through a megaphone
Each ring, a frenzy of risk.
The eyes of the audience
Oscillating—where to look,
What not to miss.

The Circus Rider

After Chagall

The red horse nods its panache,
Rolls its woman's eye.
The rider's acrobatic
Stance defies the grave

Laws of balance. Gaudy slipper hooked
Over the left shoulder. One-legged flamingo.
Right arm forming a classic gesture

Of ballet. The horse rocks on
As the full moon dangles
From a laurel branch
Like the hazardous white fruit

That can only be plucked by the angel
Flying with moth wings
Glued to a mortal body.

The circus is the sensual
Ring in which love enacts
Its risks, a production
Of gasps, thrills.

The angel's arms open wide.
It has fallen in love with a painted horse,
With the seduction of clowns.

Now it is falling
Like moonlight onto the earth,
Its wings burning off,

Its body becoming
Three rings of joy.

The Juggler

After Chagall

The freak that juggles time,
Wearing the mask of a rooster,
Crows the sun from oblivion,

Summons the earth to action.
A woman
Waltzes in her wedding gown
As if she were still a virgin.

The donkey madonna bears
The world to sorrow.

A child pivots joy
On the back of the circus pony. Hands
Grow into lilies. A man

Plays the violin as if his life
Were not simply one of many oranges
Juggled by the beaked angel.

High Wire

Who can trust the wind?
It sails the wanderer home
To a house it has demolished. You know
Its inconsistent nature:
Verb of air that won't be conjugated.

Space yawns like a mouth.
You hang by your heels to seize
A white bird falling
With the face of your ambition.

Your son nailed to a chair
Can never swerve your step
Through netless realms of air.
You test currents before gliding
With a crosspiece like a man heading
For calvary.

The errant gust as, strung between skyscrapers,
You become a pendulum
Of time gaining momentum
Until there can be no retreat. All the way down
You grip your balance pole.
It cannot bless you now.

The cable sways in heaven
Like a venomous viper or the sinuous road
Only angels risk. But your children
Will walk blindly in your footsteps,
Learning the graven shape
Of the misstep.

Clowns

See them come tumbling out of the miniature auto—
Ten, eleven, twelve, finally the midget—they're bowing, laughing,
Tripping each other. The short fat one gets a kick in the pants.
The one on stilts falls down in a clatter of bones.
One looks at us with the red woeful mouth
Of self-pity. He bawls.

Pierrot. Sad tramp.
A rubber ball nose.
Red and white lozenges. Ruff and dunce cap.
Bells on floppy toes.
Perhaps a little white dog
Who demonstrates how to waltz
On its hind legs beating
Unsupportive air with its paws.

An alarmed baby howls at the scarlet grimace.
Caterpillar eyebrows wiggling up and down. *Laugh, baby,*
Laugh
At the funny clown.
Or the sad one
With its mouth drawn down
And big tears charcoaled under its eyes

The squat man applies his clown face. *We'll have some fun.*
The boy essays a nervous laugh. *This is the handcuff trick. I do*
It just like this.

Who needs an audience?
Screams. Cries.
Now for the rope trick. Let me slip it
Around your throat
And twist. And twist.

The Chainsaw Artist

His specialty is wildlife.
The standing bear, rampant.
Eagle on a branch
Or on the wing.
He carves before an audience
Of gapers. Manhandles that
Clamorous saw to find
The animal hidden in cedar.
He's got him now. Dead in his tracks
In a dead log that provides
Life as static.
Claws raised like a threat
To the suburban lawns.

Six Acrobats and a Contortionist

A troop of double-jointed brothers
Enters cartwheeling. Flipping like
Pancakes. Walking on their hands.
Creating a pyramid as if the Sphinx
Conferred secrets of flexibility.
The youngest stands
On the shoulders of genetic
Plausibility. Watch how they
Synchronize their stunts,
A sextet of red and black tights
Like a checkerboard where each one
Kings one. Leaping sky-high
Or shuffled swiftly as a
Deck of cards. Imagine the
Endless hours of practice for
Each new trick to become automatic.
Aching muscles, pulled tendons
Perpetrating ease like a
Flight of angels.
This one: the contortionist is the most
Interesting, morphing the body's evidence
Into mystery. Impossible, you think,
To twist a language of flesh
Into such ulterior declarations.
Head between his knees, he decants
The wine and drinks. A grotesque
Gesture designed to
Repel and appeal.

The Crocodile Lady

This is her skin.
Reptilian.
Sister to lizard, alligator,
The dragons of Komodo.

She sits above you
In bra and panties
Watching you look and shudder.

Do you long to touch her?
Your squeamish urge
Leaves her cold
As the great glacier.

She is the last dinosaur,
So large with sorrow
The world cannot contain her.

The Giant

According to the old stories,
His race was first.
Their names a gargle
Of consonants.
Mountains were made for them.
They lived happy as boulders.

But the little people
Who can never let anything alone
Came armed with craft
And duplicity. Now the world is
Theirs. He thumps his head
On ceilings, bursts from clothes.
His feet hang out of beds.

His magnitude astounds them.
Their bad jokes
Bounce off his belt buckle.

He could crush them
But he won't.
The last magnanimous man.

Girl with Educated Toes

She ties a bow. Takes up
The spoon to sip
A bowl of broth. Buttons
The brass circlets of her coat,
Then plays the violin with aplomb.
All with educated toes.
Thalidomide or another
Unidentified substance
Her mother swallowed
That swallowed the buds
Of arms, leaving stubs
As if wings might have been
Hinged. With her toes, she
Picks up the pen to compose
A blessing or a curse.

Living Skeleton

Angularity of bones
Lightly strung with skin.
No fat or muscle mars
The ascetic form. An
Architecture of connections,
Of erected dreams. The body's
Pure schematic. A child says
Ain't you hungry, Mister?

Tattooed Man

Once a legitimate
Freak, back in the day
When only sailors anchored
Or centered a heart with Mother
On popeyed biceps. Dragons,
Flags, superheroes, naked ladies,
Vines, Chinese characters, geometric
Designs. Every place a needle can mine
A blaze of green, blue, lilac. Red daggers,
Black letters of a prophecy. He's been
Overtaken by a fad of frenzy,
Every Saturday-night kid with a full sleeve,
A barbwire necklace, Maori war face,
Knuckles of love and hate.
He's out of date. No tongue stud,
Nose or eyebrow ring, no
Flaunted difference—just another
Painted mausoleum.

The Lion Tamer

Sticks his head into the lion's jaws.
Rides on his back waving.
Instructs the lion to vault through fire.
Surly, in the slow obedience
Of the enslaved, the lion leaps
From perch to perch and roars.
No more whips, chairs, attitude.
Today, it's love.
The lion tamer embraces
The vast mane, the muscled haunches.
No more boots or jodhpurs. He wears
A wide-sleeved poet's shirt. Says big cats
Are his children. It's a new world. Hitches a pair
To a chariot and speeds around the ring
Like Phaethon hauling the sun
Across a sawdust sky.

The Traveling Circus

Dog and pony show is the description. An old
Benign elephant with its worn howdah.
A mangy camel and six
Little dogs that can do tricks:
Walking like a vicar on a mission,
Jumping through hoops
The way everyone has learned,
Or playing dead. The kids
Find everything funny. The ghoulish clown
Who juggles colored balls. The fattish
Lady in a spangled bathing suit
Who climbs a pole and hangs by her heels.
The tent is filled with a neighborhood
Of families seeking entertainment
Now that summer's at an end. The kids' refrain of
I'm so bored vanquished with popcorn,
Root beer, and a girl in tights
Doing handstands on a lame pony.

Circus Maximus

Even butchery
Becomes a bore. New entertainments
Are ordered. Armadas war
In a flooded arena. A fiesta of
The crucified. Long afternoons
Of blood-soaked sand.
Thumbs up or down. Caesar
Takes his time—prerogative
Of a patrician. The gaudy crowds
Eat, drink, demand more death-
Defying spectacles. More diversions.
More zany agonies.
A mob featureless except for
Mouths yelling *More! More!*
Lit with the same godfire
Of lust for suffering. They roar
With one voice as the victor
Puts the sword point to the throat,
Releasing all their bitter phlegm.
It's what they've come for.

Acknowledgments

Some of these poems have appeared in the following journals, some in earlier versions:

Abbey: "Enchantments"
Bitterzoet Magazine: "Feasts"
The Blue Bear Review: "Sword Swallower"
Broadkill Review: "Mary Mallon: Her Story"
Cat's Eye: "The Alchemist"
Chowder Review: "The Circus Rider"
Dead Snakes: "Medea"
Diverse Voices Quarterly: "Becoming Count Dracula"
First Literary Review—East: "Heidi"
The Furious Gazelle: "Vampires"
Gargoyle: "Pandora"
Grand Street: "Belle Gunness"
Grey Sparrow Journal: "Geek"
Homestead Review: "Celtic Demons"
Kentucky Review: "Tilt-A-Whirl," "Midway"
Main Street Rag: "Huck Finn"
Misfit Magazine: "Shooting Gallery," "Floyd Collins"
New Verse News: "Wallenda"
Pinyon: "Ferris Wheel"
Portland Review: "Fire Eater"
Pyrokinetics: "Roustabout"
Radiant Turnstile: "Superstitions"
Red Poppy Review: "High Wire"
Rockhurst Review: "Red Riding Hood"
Sand Canyon Review: "Dorothy"
Schuykill Valley Journal: "Ringmaster"
Silver Birch: "Brenda Starr"
The Tower Journal: "Woodman"
Vanderbilt Review: "The Juggler"
Verse Virtual: "Corn Boil"
Wisconsin Review: "Rose Red to Snow White"
Yes: A Journal of Poetry: "The Crocodile Lady," "The Fat Lady,"
     "The Giant"

"Mari Ruadh" (as "Mari Ruadh: Battle of the Birds"), "Rapunzel," and "Sleeping Beauty" first appeared in the anthology *Twice Upon a Time* (Kind of a Hurricane Press, 2015).

Cover artwork, "Praters Giant Ferris Wheel" by Letizia Barbi; author photo by Alan Colby; cover and interior book design by Diane Kistner; Georgia text and Cagliostro titling

About FutureCycle Press

FutureCycle Press is dedicated to publishing lasting English-language poetry books, chapbooks, and anthologies in both print-on-demand and Kindle ebook formats. Founded in 2007 by long-time independent editor/publishers and partners Diane Kistner and Robert S. King, the press incorporated as a nonprofit in 2012. A number of our editors are distinguished poets and writers in their own right, and we have been actively involved in the small press movement going back to the early seventies.

The FutureCycle Poetry Book Prize and honorarium is awarded annually for the best full-length volume of poetry we publish in a calendar year. Introduced in 2013, our Good Works projects are anthologies devoted to issues of universal significance, with all proceeds donated to a related worthy cause. Our Selected Poems series highlights contemporary poets with a substantial body of work to their credit; with this series we strive to resurrect work that has had limited distribution and is now out of print.

We are dedicated to giving all of the authors we publish the care their work deserves, making our catalog of titles the most diverse and distinguished it can be, and paying forward any earnings to fund more great books.

We've learned a few things about independent publishing over the years. We've also evolved a unique, resilient publishing model that allows us to focus mainly on vetting and preserving for posterity poetry collections of exceptional quality without becoming overwhelmed with bookkeeping and mailing, fundraising activities, or taxing editorial and production "bubbles." To find out more about what we are doing, come see us at www.futurecycle.org.